D1712690

THE AFRICAN AMERICAN
EXPERIENCE
FROM SLAVERY TO THE PRESIDENCY

THE
CIVIL RIGHTS
ERA

EDITED BY
HOPE LOURIE KILLCOYNE

Britannica
Educational Publishing

IN ASSOCIATION WITH

ROSEN
EDUCATIONAL SERVICES

Published in 2016 by Britannica Educational Publishing (a trademark of Encyclopædia Britannica, Inc.) in association with The Rosen Publishing Group, Inc.
29 East 21st Street, New York, NY 10010

Distributed exclusively by Rosen Publishing.
To see additional Britannica Educational Publishing titles, go to rosenpublishing.com.

First Edition

Britannica Educational Publishing
J. E. Luebering: Director, Core Reference Group
Anthony L. Green: Editor, Compton's by Britannica

Rosen Publishing
Hope Lourie Killcoyne: Executive Editor
Nelson Sá: Art Director
Nicole Russo: Designer
Cindy Reiman: Photography Manager
Introduction and supplementary material by Hope Lourie Killcoyne.

Library of Congress Cataloging-in-Publication Data

The civil rights era/edited by Hope Lourie Killcoyne.
        pages cm.—(The African American experience : from slavery to the presidency)
Includes bibliographical references and index.
ISBN 978-1-68048-048-1 (library bound)
1. African Americans—Civil rights—History—20th century. 2. Civil rights movements—United States—History—20th century. 3. United States—Race relations—20th century. I. Killcoyne, Hope Lourie, editor. II. Title: First edition.
E185.615.C5842 2015
323.1196'07309041—dc23
                                                                    2014046170

Manufactured in the United States of America

On the cover: Martin Luther King,, Jr. giving his "I Have a Dream" speech in Washington, D.C., August 28, 1963.

Photo credits: Cover, pp. 54–55 William Lovelace/Express/Hulton Archive/Getty Images; pp. 5, 49 Michael Ochs Archives/Getty Images; pp. 9, 10–11 Library of Congress Prints and Photographs Division; p. 14 Lyndon B. Johnson Library and Museum/Yoichi R. Okamoto; pp. 16–17 NARA; p. 19, 21 PhotoQuest/Archive Photos/Getty Images; pp. 22–23 Gordon Coster/The Life Picture Collection/Getty Images; p. 27 Al Gretz/FPG/Archive Photos/Getty Images; pp. 29, 36, 38–39, 46–47, 48, 60, 62–63, 66 © AP Images; p. 30 FPG/Archive Photos/Getty Images; pp. 32–33 Alfred Eisenstaedt/The Life Picture Collection/Getty Images; p. 41 Donald Uhrbrock/The Life Images Collection/Getty Images; pp. 44–45 Underwood Archives/Archive Photos/Getty Images; pp. 50–51 Library of Congress, Washington, D.C., Warren K. Leffler (digital file: cph ppmsca 03128); p. 53 Hulton Archive/Getty Images; p. 58 Frank Scherschel/The Life Picture Collection/Getty Images; p. 65 David Fenton/Archive Photos/Getty Images; p. 69 Official White House Photo by Pete Souza; interior pages background texture © iStockphoto.com/Piotr Krzeslak.

CONTENTS

INTRODUCTION

In the mid-1960s, as the United States was grappling with the civil rights struggle, many people were nonetheless more easily accepting of black music. Using the tools at hand, singer Aretha Franklin spelled out an important message to the country. Her cover of the song "Respect" topped the singles charts, becoming a lasting anthem of feminism, personal dignity, and racial equality.

What *does* respect mean in the racial sense? For starters, it means not having to drink at a "coloreds only" water fountain. Not being relegated to the back of the bus. Not having to attend a racially segregated school or play within a racially segregated sports league. Not fearing a cross burning on the lawn, a lynching in the park, or another act of violence or disrespect that might come from living in a country where most of the population was making small, medium, and huge prejudgments simply on the basis of skin color.

Respect can also begin with a name. From what is now referred to as the N word, to "boy" (even for men), to "colored," to "Negro" and "Negress," to

Aretha Franklin

"Afro-American" and "African American," to "black." And perhaps someday, when the human construct of race becomes a thing of the tarnished past, the name will simply be "American."

There is another song that broke barriers and made a crucial change in the importance of racial nomenclature: "Say it Loud—I'm Black and I'm Proud," performed by James Brown in 1968. Brown cowrote the anthemic single with his bandleader Alfred "Pee Wee" Ellis. While it was not the first time that the adjective had been used, the song's wide popularity had a huge impact. As noted in an anonymous but powerful post on the website www.portside.org:

> Up until the mid-sixties, we were trying to define ourselves: not colored anymore, now Negro. But black was not something we called ourselves. And along comes this little man and proudly states, "I'm black and I'm proud!" He took the thing that the oppressor used to bludgeon us and made it a weapon of pride for us.

But Franklin and Brown belted out their iconic songs in the late '60s, and our story begins some 30 years earlier, at the start of World War II.

During that war, black Americans increasingly sought the opportunity to fight for their country. Imagine that: petitioning the government so that you could battle— and quite possibly *die*—for a country that saw you as a second-class citizen. Not only would blacks win that fight, by the time the Vietnam War was in full swing— with American boots on the ground on the other side of the world—a disproportionate number of those boots were filled by black feet.

Through the saddest, most trying times of the mid-1900s to the beginning of a glimmer of change, there was in particular one poetic voice, one visionary leader who brought his people along the bumpy path to equality. Though he prophetically declared the possibility that he might not reach the promised land as well, Dr. Martin Luther King, Jr., was a pivotal, personable, and passionate voice that rang out in the prison of Birmingham, Alabama, and the Mall in Washington, D.C., and was finally silenced on a balcony in Memphis, Tennessee.

This book provides a short but detailed account of the black American journey from inhumane and unjust treatment to something that was beginning to look and feel like freedom. That said, some very important people in this period could not be included. So go and read about Jesse Owens making world history in the 1936 Olympics in Berlin by winning four gold medals and stunning Adolf Hitler, among others. Or learn about the multitalented writer Langston Hughes, whose poems and plays portrayed black life in America for blacks and whites alike. Or read about Shirley Chisholm, who in 1968 became the first black woman elected to the U.S. Congress. The Encyclopædia Britannica itself has excellent profiles of these and other limit-shattering leaders in the arts, athletics, and politics.

But first, read this book, *The Civil Rights Era*. It covers one of the most important chapters in American history—the path of recognition, acceptance, and lauding of one of America's greatest assets: its black American citizenry. As readers will learn, the path toward power was an often painful and protracted process, but the end result—finally being shown some of that much-deserved respect—is one that enriches us all.

CHAPTER ONE

WORLD WAR II, INDUSTRY, AND A SECOND MIGRATION

World War II began on September 1,1939, when Germany invaded Poland. By the time it ended in 1945, the war had involved nearly every part of the world.

More people died in World War II than in any other war. Experts guess that 40 to 50 million people lost their lives, many of them civilians. About six million were victims of the Holocaust—a German plan to kill people who they thought were inferior.

A little over two years after the war started, on the morning of December 7, 1941, Japanese warplanes attacked U.S. warships at the Pearl Harbor naval base in Hawaii. The airstrikes sank or crippled eight battleships, destroyed more than 180 aircraft, and killed more than 2,000 Americans. On that day, President

The *West Virginia*, burning in the foreground, was one of three battleships to sink as a result of the surprise attack on Pearl Harbor.

Franklin D. Roosevelt declared war on Japan. Soon after, war was declared on Germany, too.

But even before those declarations, the U.S. war machine had begun cranking out vehicles, weapons, tools, and supplies. By 1941, American ally Britain announced that it was fast losing the ability to pay for the war materials it had been buying from America. The U.S. Congress then gave President Roosevelt (commonly referred to as FDR) the authority to lend or lease arms and supplies to countries whose defense he deemed important to the security of the United States.

Under the Lend-Lease Act, a steady stream of planes, tanks, guns, and other war goods rolled off American assembly lines to be sent to Britain and other Allied nations. The United States, experiencing its first industrial boom in years, became known as the Arsenal of Democracy. The spike in employment was good news in the United States.

THE DEPRESSION ENDS

While that industrial boom did end the Depression, unemployed whites were generally the first to be given jobs; discrimination against blacks in hiring was rampant. Dedicated and persistent black civil rights leader and activist A. Philip Randolph felt compelled to threaten a mass protest march on Washington in order to focus nationwide attention on the widespread disparity. Alarmed at the possible consequences of such a march, which Randolph had scheduled for June 25, 1941, President Roosevelt issued Executive Order 8802, banning "discrimination in the employment of workers in defense industries or government" and establishing a Fair Employment Practices Committee (FEPC) to investigate violations. Although discrimination remained widespread, during the war blacks

A black man drinks at a water cooler for "colored" men at a streetcar terminal in Oklahoma City, Oklahoma, in 1939.

secured more jobs at better wages in a greater range of occupations than ever before.

EXECUTIVE ORDER 8802: THE BACKSTORY

Enacted by President Franklin D. Roosevelt on June 25, 1941, the very day planned for the protest march, Executive Order 8802 helped to eliminate racial discrimination in the U.S. defense industry and was an important step toward ending it in federal government employment practices overall.

Even before the Japanese attack on the U.S. naval base at Pearl Harbor, World War II had created millions of new jobs in defense industries as the United States engaged in a massive military buildup to prepare for the possibility of war. But because of discrimination in employment, black Americans gained little from this buildup, getting only the low-end jobs, if any at all.

Labor leader A. Philip Randolph, head of the Brotherhood of Sleeping Car Porters, stepped up. (At that point in America, trains were still a common and much-needed means of transportation; the now all-but-extinct porter was then largely the employment province of black men.) Randolph had long fought for black rights in employment opportunity and other realms. When the United States was preparing for war, however, President Roosevelt showed little interest in civil rights, being more concerned with having the war mobilization go smoothly and quickly. FDR was also following a political strategy of appeasing southern Democrats, who were extremely powerful in Congress and opposed federal programs aimed at uplifting African Americans.

When Randolph and other civil rights leaders tried to persuade Roosevelt to end discrimination in

BLACK LEADERS OF NOTE: A. PHILIP RANDOLPH (1889–1979)

Trade unionist and civil rights leader Asa Philip Randolph was a leading figure in the struggle for justice and parity for the black American community.

The son of a Methodist minister and a seamstress, Randolph was born in Crescent City, in the northeast corner of Florida. In 1911, he moved to Harlem, New York City. There he attended City College at night and, with journalist Chandler Owen, founded an employment agency in 1912, attempting to organize black workers. In 1917, when the United States entered World War I, the two men founded a magazine, *The Messenger* (after 1929, called *Black Worker*), which called for more positions in the war industry and the armed forces for blacks.

In 1925, Randolph became founding president of the Brotherhood of Sleeping Car Porters (BSCP). He began organizing that group and, at a time when half the affiliates of the American Federation of Labor (AFL) barred blacks from membership, he nevertheless took the BSCP into the AFL. He then went on to build the first successful black trade union, with the brotherhood winning its first major contract with the Pullman Company in 1937. (The Pullman was a "sleeping car," a luxurious railroad coach designed for overnight travel.)

(continued on the next page)

A. Philip Randolph founded the Brotherhood of Sleeping Car Porters, an African American railway union, in 1925.

(continued from the previous page)

The following year, Randolph removed his union from the AFL in protest against its failure to fight discrimination in its ranks, instead joining the newly formed Congress of Industrial Organizations (CIO). He then returned to the question of black employment in the federal government and in industries with federal contracts, leading to his threat of protest made to President Roosevelt, the result of which was Executive Order 8802.

defense-industry employment, the president initially rebuffed them. It was then that Randolph threatened to organize a large march on Washington, D.C. Roosevelt recognized that the presence of possibly 100,000 or more protesters in the capital could be embarrassing and, he felt, would distract attention from more pressing matters. In order to appease the civil rights leaders—especially Randolph—the president issued Executive Order 8802, which specified that there would be no discrimination in the U.S. defense industry on the basis of race, color, or national origin. The executive order did not establish full employment equality, but it did establish a Fair Employment Practices Committee (FEPC).

The FEPC was solely an investigative and advisory committee and lacked enforcement powers. It did, however, symbolize at least a certain level of commitment to nondiscrimination and set a precedent for the postwar civil rights achievements that occurred during the administration of Pres. Harry S. Truman. It was a step in the right direction.

EXECUTIVE ORDER

———

REAFFIRMING POLICY OF FULL PARTICIPATION IN
THE DEFENSE PROGRAM BY ALL PERSONS, REGARDLESS
OF RACE, CREED, COLOR, OR NATIONAL ORIGIN, AND
DIRECTING CERTAIN ACTION IN FURTHERANCE OF
SAID POLICY.

WHEREAS it is the policy of the United States to encourage
full participation in the national defense program by all
citizens of the United States, regardless of race, creed, color,
or national origin, in the firm belief that the democratic way
of life within the Nation can be defended successfully only with
the help and support of all groups within its borders; and

WHEREAS there is evidence that available and needed workers
have been barred from employment in industries engaged in defense
production solely because of considerations of race, creed, color,
or national origin, to the detriment of workers' morale and of
national unity:

NOW, THEREFORE, by virtue of the authority vested in me by
the Constitution and the statutes, and as a prerequisite to the
successful conduct of our national defense production effort, I
do hereby reaffirm the policy of the United States that there shall
be no discrimination in the employment of workers in defense
industries or government because of race, creed, color, or national origin, and
I do hereby declare that it is the duty of employers and of labor
organizations, in furtherance of said policy and of this order, to
provide for the full and equitable participation of all workers
in defense industries, without discrimination because of race, creed,
color, or national origin;

And it is hereby ordered as follows:

1. All departments and agencies of the Government of the
United States concerned with vocational and training programs for
defense production shall take special measures appropriate to assure
that such programs are administered without discrimination because
of race, creed, color, or national origin;

Executive Order 8802, enacted on June 25, 1941, by President
Roosevelt, helped to eliminate racial discrimination in the U.S. defense
industry. Because an executive order has the rule of law, this

- 2 -

2. All contracting agencies of the Government of the United States shall include in all defense contracts hereafter negotiated by them a provision obligating the contractor not to discriminate against any worker because of race, creed, color, or national origin;

3. There is established in the Office of Production Management a Committee on Fair Employment Practice, which shall consist of a chairman and four other members to be appointed by the President. The chairman and members of the Committee shall serve as such without compensation but shall be entitled to actual and necessary transportation, subsistence and other expenses incidental to performance of their duties. The Committee shall receive and investigate complaints of discrimination in violation of the provisions of this order and shall take appropriate steps to redress grievances which it finds to be valid. The Committee shall also recommend to the several departments and agencies of the Government of the United States and to the President all measures which may be deemed by it necessary or proper to effectuate the provisions of this order.

THE WHITE HOUSE,

June 25, 1941.

document was also an important step toward ending such discriminatory practices in federal government employment practices as a whole.

WWII

During the war, a large proportion of black soldiers overseas were in service units. Combat troops remained segregated. That said, over the course of the war, the army did introduce integrated officer training, and Benjamin O. Davis, Sr., became its first black brigadier general. His son, Benjamin O. Davis, Jr., founded a group of heroic, successful, and highly trained pilots who would begin to change the way white Americans saw black Americans and the way black Americans saw themselves. This group was the Tuskegee Airmen.

THE TUSKEGEE AIRMEN

The first African American unit of combat aviators who fought in World War II was known as the Tuskegee Airmen. They trained at Tuskegee Army Air Field in Alabama before going overseas.

General Benjamin Oliver Davis, Jr., was the founder and leader of the Tuskegee Airmen, commanding the all-black fighter squadron that began training in 1941 at the request of the Roosevelt Administration. The squadron flew missions beginning in 1943 that included shooting down enemy aircraft; bombing enemy power stations, trains, and barges; and escorting bomber groups to their missions. The Tuskegee Airmen fought in the European theater and were noted as one of the Army Air Forces' most successful and decorated escort groups. Altogether 992 pilots graduated from the Tuskegee airfield courses. They flew 1,578 missions and 15,533 sorties, destroyed 261 enemy aircraft, and won more than 850 medals.

Posters such as this one of a member of the Tuskegee Airmen were used to promote war bonds during World War II.

BLACK LEADERS OF NOTE: BENJAMIN OLIVER DAVIS, JR. (1912–2002)

American soldier Benjamin O. Davis, Jr., became the first African American general in the U.S. Air Force. His father, Benjamin O. Davis, Sr., was the first African American to become a general in any branch of the U.S. military. During World War II, Davis, Jr., led the 332nd Fighter Group—the Tuskegee Airmen—an all-black combat squadron.

Born in Washington, D.C., in 1912, Davis studied at the University of Chicago before entering the United States Military Academy at West Point, New York, in 1932. After graduating in 1936 he was commissioned in the infantry and in 1941 was among the first group of African Americans admitted to the Army Air Corps (the precursor to the U.S. Air Force) and to pilot training. Upon his graduation he was swiftly promoted to lieutenant colonel, and he organized the 99th Pursuit Squadron, the first entirely African American air unit, which flew tactical support missions in the Mediterranean theater. In 1943 he organized and commanded the Tuskegee Airmen. By the end of the war Davis himself had flown 60 combat missions and had been promoted to colonel.

After the war Davis was instrumental in desegregating the Air Force (1948) and continued to rise in rank, becoming a brigadier general (1954) and then major general (1959). Following retirement in 1970 he was named national director of civil aviation security and helped to stem a rash of aircraft hijackings in the United States. He became an assistant secretary of transportation in 1971.

Davis received many decorations during his career, including two Distinguished Service Medals and a Silver Star. On December 9, 1998, Davis was awarded his fourth general's star (making him a general of the highest order within the U.S. military). His autobiography, *Benjamin O. Davis, Jr., American*, appeared in 1991.

Benjamin Oliver Davis, Jr., is shown here in Tuskegee, Alabama, in January 1942.

In 1972 veteran Tuskegee Airmen founded Tuskegee Airmen Inc. to assist minority students with an interest in aviation and aerospace careers. They set up a trust fund that provided scholarships, and they also served as a watchdog organization overseeing the aviation industry's handling of minority issues. The 2012 film *Red Tails*, chronicling the story of the Tuskegee Airmen, was largely produced by noted filmmaker George Lucas.

World War II ended in 1945, with both the Germans and Japanese (known as the Axis powers) surrendering to the United States, Great Britain, and the other Allied nations.

In 1949, four years after the end of the war, the armed services finally adopted a policy of complete combat integration. During the Korean War, in the early 1950s, for the first time blacks fought side by side with whites in fully integrated units.

Race riots occurred during and following World War II. These African American men were rounded up following wartime race riots in Detroit, Michigan, in 1943. Army troops were called in to quell the unrest, and martial law was declared.

A SECOND MIGRATION: FROM AGRICULTURE IN THE SOUTH TO INDUSTRY IN THE NORTH

During World War II, as during World War I, there was a mass migration of blacks from the rural South. Some 1.5 million blacks left the South during the 1940s, mainly for the industrial cities of the North. Once again, serious housing shortages and job competition led to increased racial tension. Race riots broke out. The worst was in Detroit in June 1943.

Despite the riots, news of better conditions for blacks in the North and West had been spread by word of mouth as well as by reports and advertisements in African American newspapers. The influential black newspaper the *Chicago Defender* became one of the leading promoters of the Great Migration. In addition to Chicago, Illinois, other cities that absorbed large numbers of black migrants included Detroit, Michigan; Cleveland, Ohio; and New York City.

The driving factors of the Great Migration included encouraging reports of decent living conditions and jobs with good wages in the North and West. Due to labor shortages caused by immigration-curtailing laws, blacks started filling the jobs in urban industry once given to European immigrants. As noted earlier, by the time the United States joined World War II and in the decades that followed, an even greater number of jobs became available, especially in the cities, when defense industries required more unskilled labor. Again and again, large waves of

African Americans moved to Northern cities seeking employment, a better future for themselves, and the promise of a good life for their children.

Those goals notwithstanding, many blacks were not able to escape racism by migrating to the North. Rather, they were segregated into ghettos, with urban life introducing its own obstacles. Newly arriving migrants even encountered social challenges from the black establishment in the North, which tended to look down on the "country" manners of the newcomers.

CHAPTER TWO

THE CIVIL RIGHTS MOVEMENT GETS MOVING

At the end of World War II, black Americans, unwilling to give up whatever minimal gains had been made during the war, were poised to build on that base, making new and far-reaching demands to end racism. The campaign for black rights went forward in the 1940s and 1950s in persistent and deliberate steps. In the courts, the National Association for the Advancement of Colored People (NAACP), the oldest civil rights organization in the United States, having been formed in 1909, successfully attacked racially restrictive covenants in housing, segregation in interstate transportation, and discrimination in public recreational facilities.

In 1947, labor leader A. Philip Randolph founded the League for Nonviolent Civil Disobedience Against

Members of the Campaign to Resist Military Segregation protest the "Jim Crow draft," August 30, 1948, in Manhattan. Months before this march, A. Philip Randolph told the Senate Armed Services Committee, "I personally will advise Negroes to refuse to fight as slaves for a democracy they cannot possess and cannot enjoy."

Military Segregation (also known as the Committee Against Jim Crow in Military Service and Training). Aided by the success of the Tuskegee Airmen, Randolph's organization and its efforts resulted in yet another executive order, this one, number 9981, issued by President Harry S. Truman on July 26, 1948, banned segregation in the armed forces.

As the nation breathed a collective sigh of relief to have the troops back home, Americans could shift their attention once again to the national pastime: baseball. But even that arena was changing.

BLACK LEADERS OF NOTE: JACKIE ROBINSON (1919–1972)

Jackie Robinson was the first African American to play baseball in the modern era of the major leagues. He played as an infielder and outfielder for the Brooklyn Dodgers from 1947 through 1956.

Jack Roosevelt Robinson was born on January 31, 1919, in Cairo, Georgia, and grew up in Pasadena, California. He was a star athlete in football, basketball, track, and baseball at the University of California at Los Angeles. From 1942 to 1945 he served in the U.S. Army. In an episode showing signs of Robinson's future activism

Jackie Robinson steals home and New York hearts in a game against the Boston Braves on Aug. 22, 1948.

and commitment to civil rights, he faced court-martial in 1944 for refusing to follow an order that he sit at the back of a military bus. The charges against him were dismissed, and he received an honorable discharge from the military.

After leaving the Army Robinson played baseball for the Kansas City Monarchs. The team belonged to the Negro American League. At that time only white players were allowed in the major leagues.

Branch Rickey, president of the Brooklyn Dodgers, was interested in making big-league baseball open to black

(continued on the next page)

A young man outside Ebbets Field, the home of the Dodgers, shows his support for Jackie Robinson in 1947. Blacks in Brooklyn and across the nation were eager to root for Robinson and the Dodgers.

(continued from the previous page)

players. He knew that the first African American brought into the majors would have to be very special. When Rickey met Robinson, he knew he had found the right person. Robinson first played for the Dodgers in 1947. At the end of the season he was chosen as the best new player in baseball.

Although Robinson played well, things were not always easy. Players and people in the crowd often shouted hateful things at him. Pitchers sometimes threw beanballs, which means when a pitcher throws the ball at a batter's head on purpose with the intent to inflict injury. But Robinson refused to quit.

Robinson's .342 average made him the league's batting champion and most valuable player in 1949. During his career, which he spent primarily as a second baseman, Robinson helped the Dodgers capture six National League pennants and one World Series title. He retired in 1956 with a .311 lifetime batting average and 197 total stolen bases. The Dodgers later retired his number 42 jersey. When he was elected to the Baseball Hall of Fame in 1962, he was the first black player to be so honored.

After he left baseball Robinson pursued business interests while continuing to work on behalf of civil rights. Diabetes and heart problems plagued his later life, and he died on Oct. 24, 1972, in Stamford, Conn. His wife established the Jackie Robinson Foundation the following year to provide minority scholarships. In 1997, Major League Baseball held a season-long celebration marking the 50th anniversary of his historic debut.

His tombstone reads, "A life is not important except in the impact it has on other lives."

SEGREGATION

The Latin word *grex* means "flock." From it comes the word "segregation," or "to separate from the flock," meaning the separation of some people within a society from others. Separation of groups may be traditional:

Segregation in the South was documented by renowned photographer Alfred Eisenstaedt, who visited this classroom at King George High School in Fredericksburg, Virginia, in 1948.

in some religions men and women occupy different parts of a temple or mosque during worship services. Separation may also be voluntary and spontaneous: people of similar interests, values, or social status tend to associate with one another—often to the exclusion of others. Many immigrant groups in the United States, for

example, have voluntarily settled in neighborhoods with people of similar backgrounds.

"Segregation" usually refers to a system of forced separation. As such it can be either a legal or an illegal means of preserving the economic and social privileges of one group, often the majority, over others. Most frequently such separation is based on ethnic or racial differences.

In the United States segregation has affected several ethnic groups. Native American Indians were forced off their land and moved to reservations. During World War II, Japanese and Japanese Americans on the West coast were interned in what were basically concentration camps. Ten such camps were constructed to house more than 110,000 Japanese. Those who were put into the camps lost their homes, jobs, and property.

African Americans were legally segregated for a long period of time in the United States, and entrenched social, economic, and political discrimination persisted after the segregation laws were abolished. From the early 17th to the mid-19th century, large numbers of Africans were brought to the South and enslaved. After the end of Reconstruction in the late 19th century, the Southern states passed laws requiring the separation of blacks and whites in public facilities and institutions—including transportation, schools, hotels, restaurants, theaters, and other public places. These laws were declared constitutional in 1896 by the United States Supreme Court in the case *Plessy* v. *Ferguson*, which allowed for "separate but equal" public facilities.

Undoing this legal-yet-immoral segregation was not achieved until after the landmark school desegregation case—one of the most significant Supreme Court cases ever—*Brown* v. *Board of Education of Topeka*.

BROWN v. *BOARD OF EDUCATION OF TOPEKA*

In a landmark decision rendered on May 17, 1954, the U.S. Supreme Court ruled in *Brown* v. *Board of Education of Topeka* (Kansas) that racial segregation in public schools was unconstitutional. In many parts of the country, especially the South, there were separate public schools for African Americans and for whites. Throughout the South nearly all other public facilities, including parks, restaurants, railroad cars, and drinking fountains, were also separate. It was illegal for an African American to use a facility reserved for whites.

How did such acts come to be illegal? The answer is found at the close of the 19th century. In the case of *Plessy* v. *Ferguson* in 1896, Homer Plessy, who was seven-eighths white and one-eighth African American (yes, such things were measured then), purchased a rail ticket and sat in a rail car reserved for white passengers. After Plessy refused to move to a car for African Americans, he was arrested. Plessy was tried and found guilty in U.S. District Court in Louisiana, and a state supreme court upheld the verdict. The case was then taken to the U.S. Supreme Court, which ruled that laws requiring separate public facilities for African Americans and whites were constitutional as long as the facilities were approximately equal. Over half a century later, *Brown* v. *Board of Education of Topeka* overturned the "separate but equal" Plessy decision.

In Brown, the court declared that separate educational facilities for white and African American students were, in fact, inherently unequal. Although this decision strictly applied only to public schools, it implied that segregation was not permissible in other public facilities. Considered one of the most important rulings in the court's history, *Brown* v. *Board of Education of Topeka* helped to inspire the American civil rights movement of the late 1950s and 1960s. The lawyer representing the students was Thurgood Marshall, who later became the first black justice of the Supreme Court.

The Supreme Court ruled unanimously—9 to 0—in favor of the students. It found that racial segregation in public schools violated the Fourteenth Amendment to

In May 1954 the U.S. Supreme Court ruled that segregation in schools was illegal. Lawyers George Hayes (*left*), Thurgood Marshall (*center*), and James M. Nabrit (*right*) join hands outside the U.S. Supreme Court to celebrate the decision.

the Constitution. This amendment prohibits the states from denying equal protection of the laws to any person within their jurisdictions.

Writing for the court, Chief Justice Earl Warren held that even if factors such as the school buildings, the courses taught, and the qualifications of the teachers were equal, inequalities still existed between the African American and white schools. Specifically, he wrote that the policy of forcing African American children to attend separate schools solely because of their race created in them a feeling of inferiority. This feeling of inferiority undermined their motivation to learn and deprived them of educational opportunities they would enjoy in racially integrated schools. This finding, he noted, was "amply supported" by contemporary psychological research. He concluded that "in the field of public education, the doctrine of 'separate but equal' has no place. Separate educational facilities are inherently unequal."

White citizens' councils in the South fought back with legal maneuvers, economic pressure, and even violence. Rioting by white mobs temporarily closed Central High School in Little Rock, Arkansas, when nine black students were admitted to it in 1957.

A later case, commonly referred to as *Brown v. Board of Education of Topeka (II)*, was decided on May 31, 1955. It addressed what should be done to implement the decision in the first Brown case. In his opinion for the court, Warren ordered the district courts and local school authorities to take appropriate steps to integrate their public schools "with all deliberate speed." Public schools in Southern states, however, remained almost completely segregated until the late 1960s.

Black students leave the campus of Central High School in Little Rock, Arkansas, escorted by the National Guard, in September 1957. School was closing for the weekend.

The highest court in the land had validated the equality of black Americans, but the struggle was far from over. The next major sites of contention, catastrophe, and ultimate conquest were a bus, a host of lunch counters, and the capital of the United States, Washington, D.C. And who stood at the forefront of the nonviolent, eloquent, and impassioned response? The Reverend Dr. Martin Luther King, Jr.

CHAPTER THREE

MARTIN LUTHER KING, JR., AND THE CIVIL RIGHTS MOVEMENT

Inspired by the belief that love and peaceful protest could eliminate social injustice, Martin Luther King, Jr., became one of the outstanding black leaders in the United States. He inspired whites and blacks alike to protest racial discrimination, poverty, and war through nonviolent resistance to oppression.

EARLY LIFE

Martin Luther King, Jr., was born in Atlanta, Georgia, on January 15, 1929. His father, Martin, Sr., was the pastor of the Ebenezer Baptist Church, a black

Martin Luther King, Jr., speaks against discrimination at a student rally in Alabama.

congregation. His mother, Alberta Williams King, was a schoolteacher. Martin had an older sister, Christine, and a younger brother, Alfred Daniel.

Martin encountered racism at an early age. When he was six, his friendship with two white playmates was cut short by their parents. When he was 11, a white woman hit him and called him a nigger.

Martin was admitted to Morehouse College at 15, without having completed high school. He decided to become a minister and at 18 was ordained in his father's church. After graduating from Morehouse in 1948, he entered Crozer Theological Seminary in Chester, Pennsylvania. He was the valedictorian of his class in 1951 and won a graduate fellowship. At Boston University he received a Ph.D. in theology in 1955.

In Boston King met Coretta Scott. They were married in 1953 and had two sons and two daughters.

THE MONTGOMERY BUS BOYCOTT

King had been impressed by the teachings of Henry David Thoreau and Mahatma Gandhi on nonviolent resistance. King wrote, "I came to feel that this was the only morally and practically sound method open to oppressed people in their struggle for freedom." He became pastor of the Dexter Avenue Baptist Church in Montgomery, Alabama, in 1954.

King had been pastor of that church slightly more than a year when the city's small group of civil rights advocates decided to contest racial segregation on their public bus system. The impetus? On December 1, 1955, Rosa Parks, a black woman, had refused to surrender her bus seat to a white passenger. The consequence? Parks was arrested for violating the city's segregation law. So activists formed the Montgomery Improvement Association to boycott the transit system and chose King as their leader. In his first speech to the group as its president, King declared:

> We have no alternative but to protest. For many years we have shown an amazing patience. We have sometimes given our white brothers the feeling that we liked the way we were being treated. But we come here tonight to be saved from that patience that makes us patient with anything less than freedom and justice.

These words, gaining nationwide attention, introduced to the country a fresh voice, a skillful rhetoric, an inspiring personality, and in time, a dynamic new doctrine of civil struggle. Although King's home was dynamited and his family's safety threatened, he continued to lead the boycott until, late in 1956, the United States Supreme Court forced desegregation of the buses. King believed that the boycott proved that "there is a new Negro in the South, with a new sense of dignity and destiny." To coordinate further civil rights action, the Southern Christian Leadership Conference (SCLC) was established in 1957 under King's leadership. Also in that year, King became the youngest recipient of the Spingarn Medal, an award presented annually to an outstanding black person by the NAACP.

A visit to India in 1959 gave King a long-awaited opportunity to study inspirational Indian leader Mahatma Gandhi's techniques of nonviolent protest.

BLACK LEADERS OF NOTE: ROSA PARKS (1913–2005)

By refusing to give up her bus seat to a white man in the segregated South, Rosa Parks sparked the United States civil rights movement. Her action led to the 1955–56 Montgomery, Alabama, bus boycott, and she became a symbol of the power of nonviolent protest.

Rosa Louise McCauley was born on February 4, 1913, in Tuskegee, Alabama. She briefly attended Alabama State Teachers College (now Alabama State University) and in 1932 married Raymond Parks, a barber. She worked as a seamstress and became active in the NAACP, serving as secretary of the Montgomery chapter from 1943 to 1956.

On her way home from work one day in 1955, Parks was told by a bus driver to surrender her seat to a white man. Refusing to do so, she was arrested and fined. She was also fired from her job and threatened by white people, so in 1957 she and her family moved to Detroit, Michigan. She then worked in the office of U.S. Representative John Conyers, Jr. She was honored with two of the country's highest civilian awards: the Presidential Medal of Freedom in 1996, and the Congressional Gold Medal of Honor in 1999. Rosa Parks died in Detroit on October 24, 2005.

Rosa Parks rides a bus in Montgomery, Alabama, in 1956.

In 1958 a group of black children take part in a protest against a restaurant in Oklahoma. The restaurant had refused to serve blacks.

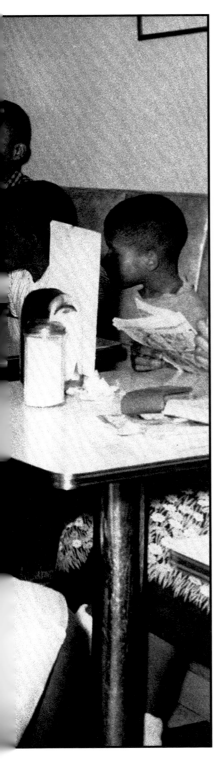

In 1960 King became copastor of his father's church in Atlanta. The next year he led a "nonviolent army" to protest discrimination in Albany, a city in southwestern Georgia.

THE CIVIL RIGHTS MOVEMENT GATHERS STEAM

Within 15 years after the Supreme Court outlawed all-white primary elections in 1944, the registered black electorate in the South increased more than fivefold, reaching 1,250,000 in 1958. The Civil Rights Act of 1957, the first federal civil rights legislation to be passed since 1875, authorized the federal government to take legal measures to prevent any citizen from being denied voting rights.

With that victory in hand, it was time to tackle some day-to-day issues. Beginning in February 1960 in Greensboro, North Carolina, student sit-ins forced the desegregation of lunch counters in drug and variety

A young black man holds his own sit-in at a lunch counter in Tampa, Florida, 1960. Part of a larger group organized by the NAACP that went into stores and luncheonettes alone or in pairs, he—as well as the others—was indeed served his requested meal.

stores throughout the South. In April of that year leaders of the sit-in movement organized the Student Nonviolent Coordinating Committee (SNCC). The following spring, the Freedom Rides, intended to both defy and bring national attention to the practice of segregation on interstate buses in Alabama and Mississippi, were organized by the Congress of Racial Equality (CORE) under its national director, civil rights activist James Farmer.

FREEDOM NOW

Blacks adopted Freedom Now as their slogan to recognize the Emancipation Proclamation's centennial in 1963, which would prove to be an event-filled year for the movement. National attention that spring was focused on Birmingham, Alabama, where King was leading a civil rights drive to desegregate many public facilities there. The Birmingham authorities used dogs and fire hoses

In Birmingham, Alabama, firefighters use a water cannon against black children to break up a May 1963 civil rights demonstration organized by Reverend Dr. Martin Luther King, Jr.

to quell civil rights demonstrators, and there were mass arrests.

LETTER FROM BIRMINGHAM JAIL

King was jailed along with large numbers of his supporters, including hundreds of schoolchildren. But not all blacks, notably including some members of the clergy, supported King. Further, he was strongly opposed by some members of the white clergy, who issued a statement urging African Americans not to support the demonstrations. In a moving appeal known as the Letter from Birmingham Jail, King argued that Asian and African nations were fast achieving political independence while "we still creep at a horse-and-buggy pace toward gaining a cup of coffee at a lunch counter."

THE MARCH ON WASHINGTON

Near the end of the Birmingham campaign, in an effort to draw together the multiple forces for peaceful change and to dramatize to the country and the world the

Civil rights supporters carry placards at the March on Washington, D.C., on August 28, 1963.

importance of solving the U.S. racial problem, King joined other civil rights leaders in organizing the historic March on Washington. On August 28, 1963, an interracial assembly of more than 200,000 gathered peaceably in the shadow of the Lincoln Memorial to demand equal justice for all citizens under the law. Here the crowds were uplifted by the emotional strength and prophetic quality of King's famous "I Have a Dream" speech, in which he emphasized his faith that all men, someday, would be brothers.

At the national level, the March on Washington helped secure the passage of the Civil Rights Act of

16TH STREET BAPTIST CHURCH BOMBING

King's clarity and eloquence notwithstanding, less than a month later, on September 15, 1963, a bomb was thrown into a predominantly black church in Birmingham, Alabama. The terrorist attack, which occurred during Sunday school classes just before the church service was to begin, was the work of local Ku Klux Klan (KKK) members. Resulting in 14 injuries and the death of four girls, the attack garnered widespread national outrage. Decades later, director Spike Lee's 1997 documentary *4 Little Girls* includes interviews with witnesses to the bombing and family members of the victims. It also explores the segregation and white harassment that were central to the time period.

1964, which forbade discrimination in voting, public accommodations, and employment and permitted the attorney general of the United States to deny federal funds to local agencies that practiced discrimination. Efforts to increase the black vote were also helped by the ratification in 1964 of the Twenty-Fourth Amendment to the Constitution, which banned the poll tax. This was a practice in which many people were required to make a payment piror to registering to vote. Many poor blacks, unable to pay for this prerequisite to voting, were denied the right to vote. King also became the youngest recipient of the Nobel Peace Prize in 1964.

An organizer for the NAACP, Medgar Evers, shown here in about 1955, was murdered in Jackson, Mississippi, in 1963. The case received national attention.

Martin Luther King, Jr., and Coretta Scott King (*right*) lead the march for voting rights in 1965 from Selma to Montgomery, Alabama. The march included some 40,000 protesters.

SELMA: A BRIDGE TOO FAR?

The first signs of opposition to King's tactics from within the civil rights movement itself surfaced during the March 1965 demonstrations in Selma, Alabama, which were aimed at dramatizing the need for a federal voting-rights law that would provide legal support for the enfranchisement of Southern blacks. King organized an initial march from Selma to the state capitol in Montgomery but did not lead it himself. The marchers were turned back by state troopers who attacked them with nightsticks and tear gas.

King was determined to lead a second march, despite an injunction by a federal court and efforts from Washington to persuade him to cancel it. Heading a procession of 1,500 marchers, black and white, he set out across Pettus Bridge outside Selma until the group came to a barricade of state troopers. But instead of going on and forcing a confrontation, he led his followers to kneel in prayer and then unexpectedly turned back. This decision cost King the support of many young radicals who were already faulting him for being too cautious. The suspicion of an "arrangement" with federal and local authorities—vigorously but not entirely convincingly denied—clung to the Selma affair. The country was nevertheless aroused, resulting in the passage of the Voting Rights Act of 1965.

CHAPTER FOUR

ANOTHER WAR, THE BLACK REVOLT, AND THE DEATH OF A DREAMER

The Vietnam War, in which black soldiers participated in disproportionately high numbers, tended to divide the black leadership and divert white liberals from the civil rights movement. Some NAACP and National Urban League leaders minimized the war's impact on the black home front. A tougher view—that U.S. participation had become a racist intrusion in a nonwhite nation's affairs—was shared by other black leaders, including King. He believed that the money and effort spent on war could be used to combat poverty and discrimination. King also felt that he would be a hypocrite if he protested racial violence without condemning the violence of war, as well.

But militant black leaders began to attack King's appeals for nonviolence. They accused him of being influenced too much by whites. Simultaneously, government officials criticized his "peacenik" stand on Vietnam. Some black leaders felt that King's statements against war diverted public attention from civil rights. Some blacks turned toward a more aggressive stance to rectify their position in American society.

BLACK NATIONALISM: MALCOLM X AND THE NATION OF ISLAM

A black militant, Malcolm X championed the rights of African Americans and urged them to develop racial unity. He was known for his association first with the Nation of Islam, sometimes known as the Black Muslims, and later with the Organization of Afro-American Unity, which he founded after breaking with the Nation of Islam.

Malcolm Little was born in Omaha, Nebraska, on May 19, 1925, the seventh of eleven children. The family soon moved to Lansing, Michigan. There they were harassed by whites who resented the black nationalist views of Malcolm's father, Earl Little, an organizer for a "back-to-Africa" movement.

When Malcolm was six his father was murdered. His mother later suffered a nervous breakdown, and the family was separated by welfare agencies. Later in

Malcolm X addresses an annual Muslim convention in Chicago, Illinois, in February 1961.

his life Malcolm came to believe that white people had destroyed his family. In eighth grade he dropped out of school. As a young man he moved to Boston and became involved in crime. Arrested and sent to prison for robbery, it was while incarcerated that he learned of a group called the Nation of Islam. This organization followed some of the teachings of Islam. It also taught that blacks were superior to whites.

Little joined the Nation of Islam in 1952. He gave up his last name because it was the one that slaveholders had given to his ancestors. He replaced it with an *X*, which stood for his unknown African family name.

An articulate and charismatic public speaker, from 1955 to 1965 Malcolm X expressed the pent-up anger, frustration, and bitterness of black Americans. He preached on the streets of Harlem and spoke at major universities such as Harvard. His keen intellect, incisive wit, and ardent radicalism made him a formidable critic of American society. He also criticized the mainstream civil rights movement, challenging Martin Luther King's core beliefs of integration and nonviolence. Malcolm argued that more was at stake than the civil right to sit in a restaurant or even to vote; he felt that the most important issues were actually black identity, integrity, and independence. In contrast to King's strategy of nonviolence, civil disobedience, and redemptive suffering, Malcolm X urged his followers to defend themselves "by any means necessary." His biting critique of the "so-called Negro" provided the intellectual foundations for the Black Power and black consciousness movements of the late 1960s and '70s. Through the influence of the Nation of Islam, Malcolm

Black Olympians Tommie Smith (*center*) and John Carlos give the Black Power salute at the 1968 Olympics as the U.S. national anthem is played.

X helped to change the terms used to refer to African Americans from "Negro" and "colored" to "black" and "Afro-American."

But all was not well within the leadership of the Nation of Islam itself. In 1964, after long and bitter tensions and disagreements with the organization's founder, Elijah Muhammad, Malcolm X left the movement. He then converted to traditional Islam and took the name el-Hajj Malik el-Shabazz. During his pilgrimage to Mecca, Saudi Arabia, that same year, he changed his views about whites. He also broadened his focus from civil rights to include human rights. Unfortunately, those new beliefs angered some in the Nation of Islam, to the extent that on February 21, 1965, when he was speaking in New York City, he was shot and killed. Three members of the Nation of Islam were convicted of his murder.

As for King, by 1965, he, too, was dispirited that the progress of civil rights in the South had not been matched by improvements in the lives of Northern blacks. In response to the riots in poverty-stricken black urban neighborhoods in 1965, he was determined to focus America's attention on the living conditions of blacks in Northern cities. In 1966 he established a headquarters in a Chicago, Illinois, slum apartment. From this base he organized protests against the city's discrimination in housing and employment.

INNER-CITY VIOLENCE ERUPTS

During this tumultuous time, some of the nation's other black-inhabited inner cities were swept by violent outbreaks. Their basic causes were long-standing grievances—police insensitivity and

THE BLACK PANTHER PARTY

The Black Panthers were a revolutionary party founded in 1966 in Oakland, California, by radical political activists Huey Newton and Bobby Seale. The party's original purpose was to patrol black neighborhoods to protect residents from acts of police brutality.

The Panthers eventually developed into a Marxist revolutionary group that called for the arming of all black Americans, the exemption of blacks from the draft and from all sanctions of white America, the release of all black Americans from jail, and the payment of compensation to blacks for centuries of exploitation by whites.

As the party grew, finding allies both within and beyond the borders of the United States, the organization also found itself squarely in the crosshairs of the Federal Bureau of Investigation (FBI). In fact, in 1969 FBI director J. Edgar Hoover considered the Black Panther Party to be the greatest threat to national security.

Black Panther Party national chairman Bobby Seale (*left*) and defense minister Huey Newton guard the party headquarters in Oakland, California.

brutality, inadequate educational and recreational facilities, high unemployment, poor housing, and high prices. Yet the outbreaks were mostly unplanned. Unlike the race riots of earlier decades, the outbreaks of the 1960s involved the looting and burning of white-owned property in black neighborhoods. The fighting that took place was mainly between young black men and the police. Hundreds of lives were lost and tens of millions of dollars' worth of property was destroyed. The most serious disturbances occurred in the Watts area of Los Angeles, California, in July 1965 and in Newark, New Jersey, and Detroit, Michigan, in July 1967.

The mid-1960s were thus a time ripe for militant black nationalist and Marxist-oriented black organizations, among them the Revolutionary Action Movement, the Deacons for Defense, and, the best-known of all, the Black Panther Party. Under such leaders as civil rights activists Stokely Carmichael and H. Rap Brown, even the Student Nonviolent Coordinating Committee (SNCC) adopted more radical policies, its very name and history notwithstanding.

BLACK POWER

The slogan Black Power became popular in the late 1960s. It was first used by Carmichael in June 1966 during a civil rights march in Mississippi. However, the concept of black power predated the slogan. Essentially, it referred to all attempts by American blacks to maximize their political and economic power.

A mother and her family receive medical care at a Black Panther community health care clinic in Chicago, Illinois, in 1969.

The black power movement was stimulated by the growing pride of black Americans in their African heritage. This pride was symbolized most strikingly by the Afro hairstyle and the African garments worn by many young blacks. Black pride was also manifested in student demands for black studies programs, black teachers, and an upsurge in African American creative arts. The new slogan—updated from Harlem Renaissance poet Langston Hughes— was Black Is Beautiful.

The tombstone of the Reverend Dr. Martin Luther King, Jr., is shown here along with its image in a reflecting pool at the Martin Luther King Jr. National Historic Site in Atlanta, Georgia. Coretta Scott King was interred alongside her husband after her death in 2006.

THE DEATH OF A DREAMER

Ever the voice of nonviolent protest, in 1968 King planned the Poor People's Campaign, a march on Washington, D.C., to dramatize the relationship of poverty to urban violence. Unfortunately, he did not live to take part in it. Early in 1968 he traveled to Memphis, Tennessee, to support a strike of poorly paid sanitation workers. There, on April 4, he was assassinated by a sniper, James Earl Ray, who was eventually tried and convicted of the murder.

King's death shocked the nation and, ironically, given his stance on violence, precipitated rioting by blacks in many cities. He was buried in Atlanta under a monument inscribed with the final words of his famous "I Have a Dream" speech. Taken from an old slave song, the inscription reads:

Free at Last, Free at Last,
Thank God Almighty
I'm Free at Last.

In 1977 King was posthumously awarded the Presidential Medal of Freedom for his battle against prejudice. In 1986 the United States Congress established a national holiday in King's honor to be observed on the third Monday in January.

CONCLUSION

Despite the gains made by black Americans through the civil rights movement and its more radical offshoots, housing and therefore educational segregation still persists in various regions—from rural to urban—in the United States. The Fair Housing Act passed by Congress in 1968 made residential segregation a federal offense. But this law applies only when local laws are used to create or maintain segregated neighborhoods. In some cases, segregation is maintained by factors other than local laws. For example, blacks who want to buy homes in white neighborhoods may be steered away by real estate agents.

That said, the most famous house in America—the White House—was occupied for two terms by a black president, Barack Hussein Obama, beginning in 2009. And that's not nothing. It is, in fact, quite worthy of respect.

President Barack Obama is shown in the Oval Office on Thanksgiving Day, 2011, making calls to several U.S. military service members in the Army, the Air Force, the Coast Guard, the Marine Corps, and the Navy. He thanked them for their service overseas and wished them a happy Thanksgiving.

TIMELINE

1939

World War II begins on September 1, when Germany invades Poland.

1941

Japan attacks Pearl Harbor on December 7. The United States declares war on Japan and soon after on Germany.

1941

Issued by President Franklin D. Roosevelt, Executive Order 8802 bans "discrimination in the employment of workers in defense industries or government" and establishes a Fair Employment Practices Committee (FEPC) to investigate violations.

1947

Jackie Robinson becomes the first African American athlete to play in baseball's major leagues in the 20th century.

1953

Ralph Ellison's novel *Invisible Man* wins the National Book Award.

1954

In a landmark decision rendered on May 17, the U.S. Supreme Court rules in *Brown* v. *Board of Education of Topeka* that racial segregation in public schools is unconstitutional. In other words, separate is not equal.

1955

Marian Anderson becomes the first black person to sing at the Metropolitan Opera House.

1955

In Montgomery, Alabama, Rosa Parks refuses to give up her bus seat to a white man. Activists form the Montgomery Improvement Association to boycott the transit system, choosing 26-year-old pastor Martin Luther King, Jr., as their leader.

1956

Singer and pianist Nat King Cole becomes the first black entertainer with a network television series. It runs for a year. (Klan members had set a burning cross on the lawn of his Los Angeles home in 1948.)

1963

King leads a civil rights drive to desegregate many public facilities in Birmingham, Alabama. Arrested and jailed, he writes the seminal work of nonviolent activism, Letter from Birmingham Jail.

1963

King and other civil rights leaders organize the historic March on Washington, an interracial assembly of more than 200,000 that gathered peaceably in the shadow of the Lincoln Memorial to demand equal justice for all citizens under the law.

1963

The 16th Street Church in Birmingham, Alabama, is bombed by the KKK. Four young girls are killed.

1965

King leads a march from Selma, Alabama, to the state's capital, Montgomery, March 21–25. The march was the final event of several tumultuous weeks during which demonstrators twice attempted to march but were stopped—once violently—by local police. As many

as 25,000 people participated in the roughly 50-mile (80 km) march.

1966

The Black Panther Party is founded.

1967

Aretha Franklin, the newly crowned "Queen of Soul," records the song "Respect," a dazzling and arresting cover of Otis Redding's spirited compostition.

1968

Dr. Martin Luther King, Jr., is assassinated in Memphis, Tennessee.

GLOSSARY

ANTHEM Song of praise or happiness.

BLACK NATIONALIST Member of a group of militant blacks who advocate separatism from whites and the formation of self-governing black communities.

BRIGADIER Military commissioned officer with a rank just below major general.

ENFRANCHISEMENT The granting of full privileges of citizenship, especially the right to vote.

EXECUTIVE ORDER Order issued by the president of the United States (to the army, navy, or another part of the executive branch of the government) that has the force of law.

INJUNCTION Court order commanding or forbidding the doing of some act (such as a strike, a demonstration, or a march).

JIM CROW The name comes from a once-popular stage performance that began in the early 1800s. Called minstrel shows, they involved lively entertainment that encouraged a negative view of blacks. The term "Jim Crow" became an unfavorable name for blacks as well as a term for their segregation. The anti-black laws that were in place in the South from the late 1870s until the 1950s were known as Jim Crow laws.

KU KLUX KLAN (KKK) Terrorist group that formed after the Civil War ended in 1865. The Klan's goal was to reestablish the dominance of the prewar plantation aristocracy. It was revived in an altered form in the 20th century.

LYNCHING Form of violence in which a mob, under the pretext of administering justice without trial, executes a presumed offender, often after inflicting torture and mutilation.

MARXIST One who follows the socialist ideas of 19th-century German philosopher Karl Marx. (The goal of socialism being to spread wealth more evenly and to treat all people fairly.)

PEACENIK Coined in 1962, one who opposes war, specifically, one who participates in antiwar demonstrations.

PILGRIMAGE The journey one takes to a shrine or sacred place.

RADICAL One who favors rapid and sweeping changes, especially in laws and methods of government.

RECONSTRUCTION The reorganization and reestablishment of the Confederate states in the Union after the American Civil War.

RHETORIC The skillful use of words to persuade or influence others. The term comes from a Greek word meaning "orator."

SANCTIONS Actions taken to enforce a law or rule.

SORTIES Sudden rushing out of troops from positions of defense against an enemy.

SQUADRON Any of several units of military organization.

THEOLOGY The study of religion.

FOR MORE INFORMATION

African American Museum in Philadelphia (AAMP)

701 Arch Street

Philadelphia, PA 19106

(215) 574-0380

Website: www.aampmuseum.org

The exhibits at the AAMP chronicle the political, social, cultural, and artistic history of African Americans from precolonial times to the present. Its collections and artifacts help preserve African American heritage and its traditions.

British Columbia Black History Awareness Society (BCHAS)

216 Michigan Street

Victoria, BC V8V 1R3

Canada

Website: www.islandnet.com/~bcbhas/index.html

The British Columbia Black History Awareness Society (BCBHAS) was created in 1994 to heighten awareness of the history and contributions of Black history in British Columbia.

National Association for the Advancement of Colored People (NAACP)

National Headquarters

4805 Mt. Hope Drive

Baltimore, MD 21215

Toll Free: (877) NAACP-98

Website: www.naacp.org

Since 1909 the National Association for the Advancement of Colored People (NAACP) has been advocating for rights for all, as well as striving to eliminate discrimination based on race.

National Coalition of 100 Black Women

1925 Adam C. Powell Jr. Blvd.

Suite 1L

New York, NY 10026

(212) 222-5660

Website: www.ncbw.org

The National Coalition of 100 Black Women is a nonprofit, volunteer-run organization that supports all women and strives for racial and gender equality.

National Urban League

120 Wall Street

New York, NY 10005

(212) 558-5300

Website: nul.iamempowered.com

Founded during the Great Migration, the National Urban League continues its long tradition of empowering underserved communities. The organization supports initiatives in education, employment, housing, and health care and advocates for civil rights.

North American Black Historical Museum

277 King Street

Amherstburg, ON N9V 2C7

Canada

(519) 736-5433

Website: www.blackhistoricalmuseum.org

The artifacts preserved and presented by the North American Black Historical Museum tell the story of African Canadians through the centuries. Visitors can tour the museum's collections or participate in one of its numerous events.

Schomburg Center for Research in Black Culture

515 Malcolm X Boulevard

New York, NY 10037

(917) 275-6975

Website: www.nypl.org/locations/schomburg

This research arm of the New York Public Library is committed to researching, documenting, and preserving African American history and culture. Visitors can explore its collections or access its many resources for research purposes.

WEBSITES

Because of the changing nature of Internet links, Rosen Publishing has developed an online list of websites related to the subject of this book. This site is updated regularly. Please use this link to access this list:

http://www.rosenlinks.com/AAE/Right

BIBLIOGRAPHY

Aretha, David. *Martin Luther King Jr. and the 1963 March on Washington.* Greensboro, NC: Morgan Reynolds Publishing, 2014

Berlin, Ira. *The Making of African America: The Four Great Migrations.* New York, NY: Penguin, 2010.

Hansen, Joyce. *Women of Hope: African Americans Who Made a Difference.* New York, NY: Scholastic, 2007.

King, Martin Luther, Jr., and Clayborne Carson. *The Autobiography of Martin Luther King, Jr.* New York, NY: Intellectual Properties Management in association with Warner Books, 1998.

Myers, Walter Dean. *Malcolm X: By Any Means Necessary.* New York, NY: Scholastic, 1994.

Philips, Kimberly L. *War! What Is It Good For? Black Freedom Struggles and the U.S. Military from World War II to Iraq.* Chapel Hill, NC: The University of North Carolina Press, 2012.

Plummer, Brenda Gayle. *In Search of Power: African Americans in the Era of Decolonization, 1956-1974.* New York, NY: Cambridge University Press, 2014.

Reich, Steven A., ed. *The Great Black Migration: A Historical Encyclopedia of the American Mosaic.* Santa Barbara, CA: ABC-CLIO, 2014.

Wakin, Edward. *At the Edge of Harlem: Portrait of a Middle-Class Negro Family.* New York, NY: William Morrow, 1965.

Wiggins, D. K., ed. *Out of the Shadows: A Biographical History of African American Athletes.* Fayetteville, AK: University of Arkansas Press, 2006.

INDEX